Part 3

Student
Activity
Book 3

PEARSON

Scott
Foresman

scottforesman.com

Editorial Offices: Glenview, Illinois • Parsippany, New Jersey • New York, New York
Sales Offices: Boston, Massachusetts • Duluth, Georgia • Glenview, Illinois
Coppell, Texas • Sacramento, California • Mesa, Arizona

ISBN: 0-328-26052-5

Copyright © Pearson Education, Inc.

All Rights Reserved. Printed in the United States of America. All content in this publication is protected by Copyright. The blackline masters are designed for use with appropriate equipment to reproduce copies for classroom use only. Scott Foresman grants permission to classroom teachers to reproduce from these masters.

15 16 17 V001 15 14

Table of Contents

Writer's Warm-Up

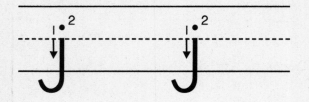

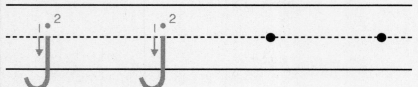

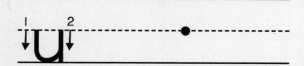

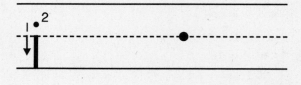

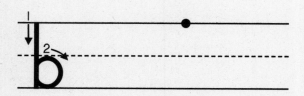

© Pearson Education, Inc.

Word Maze

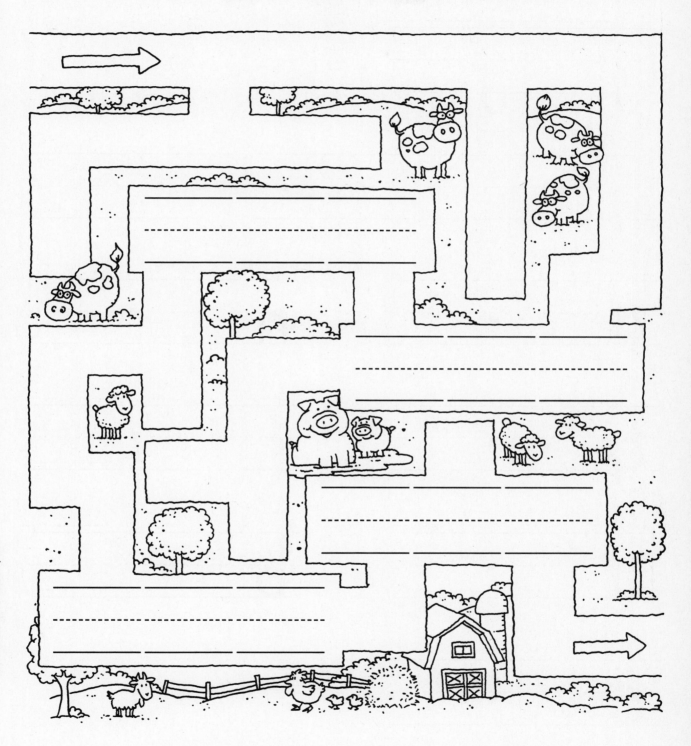

© Pearson Education, Inc.

Name _____

Writer's Warm-Up

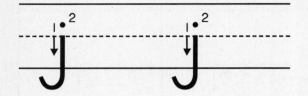

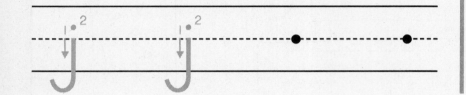

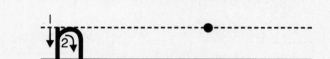

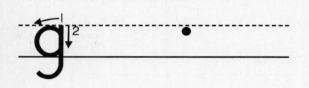

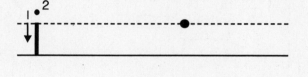

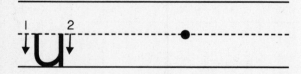

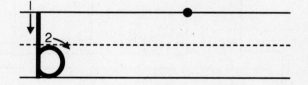

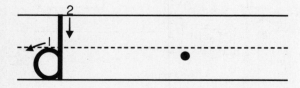

© Pearson Education, Inc.

Activity 5

Word Race

© Pearson Education, Inc.

Name _____

Writer's Warm-Up

W W

W W • •   • •

a •   n •

g •   i •

u •   j •

b •

Activity 5

© Pearson Education, Inc.

Name _____

Writer's Warm-Up

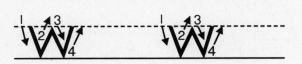

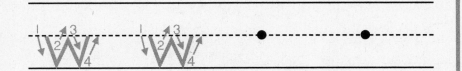

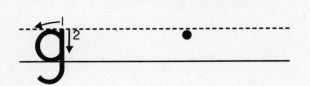

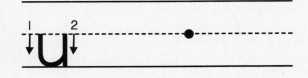

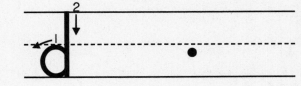

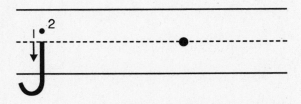

© Pearson Education, Inc.

Name _____

Jack and the Beanstalk

© Pearson Education, Inc.

Name _____

Treasure Hunt

© Pearson Education, Inc.

_____ _____ _____

- - - - - - - - - - - - - - - -

_____ _____ _____

_____ _____ _____

- - - - - - - - - - - - - - - -

_____ _____ _____

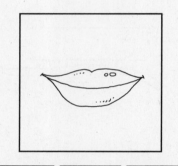

_____ _____ _____

- - - - - - - - - - - - - - - -

_____ _____ _____

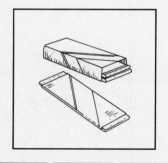

_____ _____ _____

- - - - - - - - - - - - - - - -

_____ _____ _____

_____ _____ _____

- - - - - - - - - - - - - - - -

_____ _____ _____

© Pearson Education, Inc.

Name _____

Writer's Warm-Up

e   e

e   e   •   • | •   •

w   n

g   i

u   j

b

© Pearson Education, Inc.

Activity 5

13

Writer's Warm-Up

e   *e*

e   *e*   •   • | •   •

w   •   *n*   •

g   •   *b*   •

u   •   *d*   •

j   •

© Pearson Education, Inc.

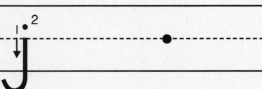

Activity 5

14

Word Writing Game

_____ _____ _____

- - - - - - - - - - - - - - - - - -

_____ _____ _____

_____ _____ _____

- - - - - - - - - - - - - - - - - -

_____ _____ _____

_____ _____ _____

- - - - - - - - - - - - - - - - - -

_____ _____ _____

_____ _____ _____

- - - - - - - - - - - - - - - - - -

_____ _____ _____

_____ _____ _____

- - - - - - - - - - - - - - - - - -

_____ _____ _____

_____ _____ _____

- - - - - - - - - - - - - - - - - -

_____ _____ _____

© Pearson Education, Inc.

Guess What I Am

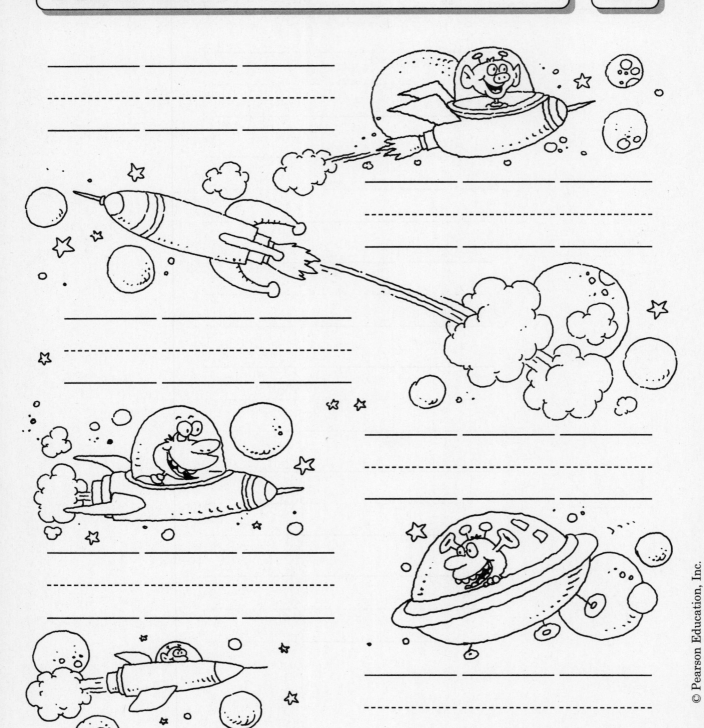

_____ _____ _____

- -

_____ _____ _____

_____ _____ _____

- -

_____ _____ _____

Activity 7

© Pearson Education, Inc.

Name _____

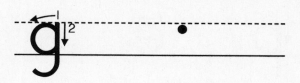

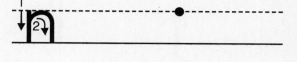

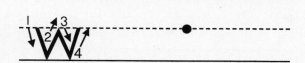

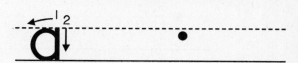

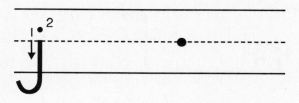

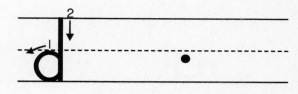

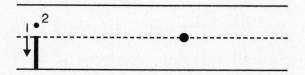

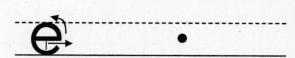

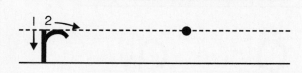

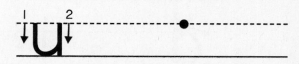

© Pearson Education, Inc.

Writer's Warm-Up

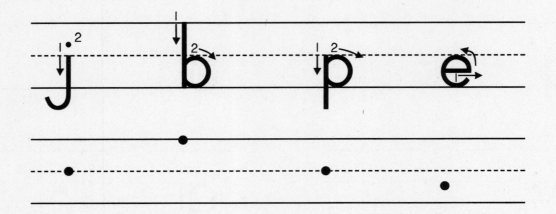

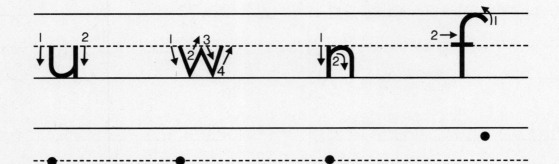

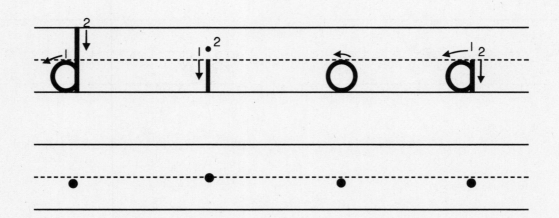

© Pearson Education, Inc.

Name _____

Treasure Hunt

© Pearson Education, Inc.

Name _____

Word Page

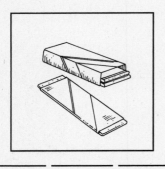

___ ___ ___

- - - - - - - - - - - - - - - - - -

___ ___ ___

___ ___ ___

- - - - - - - - - - - - - - - - - -

___ ___ ___

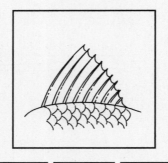

___ ___ ___

- - - - - - - - - - - - - - - - - -

___ ___ ___

___ ___ ___

- - - - - - - - - - - - - - - - - -

___ ___ ___

___ ___ ___

- - - - - - - - - - - - - - - - - -

___ ___ ___

© Pearson Education, Inc.

Name _____

Writer's Warm-Up

z z

z z • • | • •

w •   n •

g •   e •

u •   j •

b •

© Pearson Education, Inc.

Name _____

Writer's Warm-Up

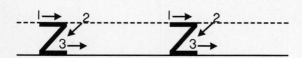

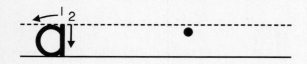

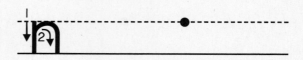

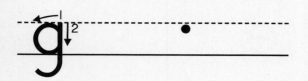

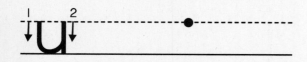

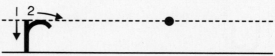

© Pearson Education, Inc.

Name _____

Rescue the Cat

© Pearson Education, Inc.

Name _____

Writer's Warm-Up

Lesson
88

h   h

h   h

z   n

g   w

e   b

j

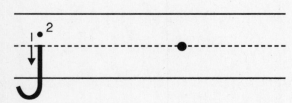

Activity 5

24

© Pearson Education, Inc.

Writer's Warm-Up

h   h

h   h

z   n

g   w

u   r

j

© Pearson Education, Inc.

Silly Words

© Pearson Education, Inc.

Writer's Warm-Up

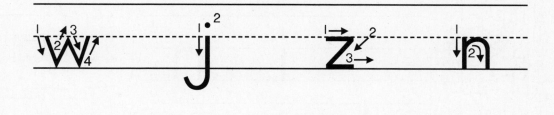

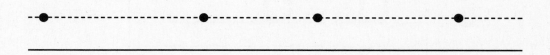

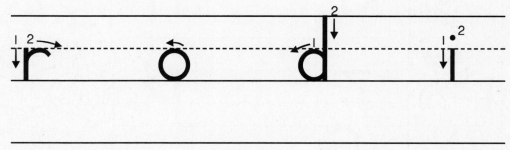

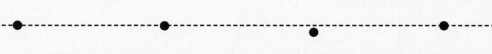

© Pearson Education, Inc.

Missing Letters

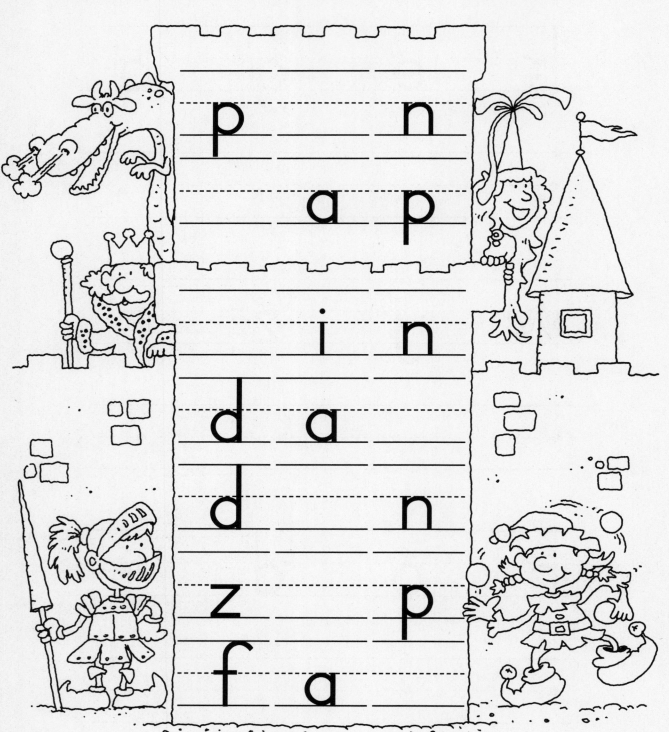

p ___ n
___ a p

___ ___ ___
___ i n
d ___ a
d ___ n
z ___ p
f a ___

© Pearson Education, Inc.

Name _____

Writer's Warm-Up

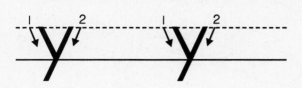

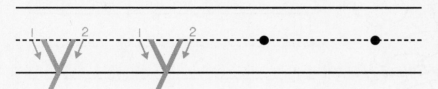

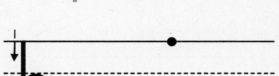

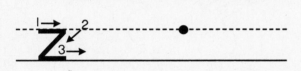

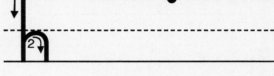

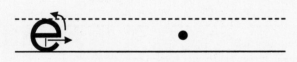

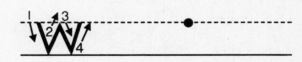

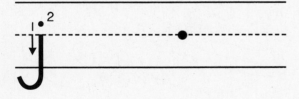

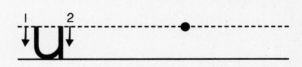

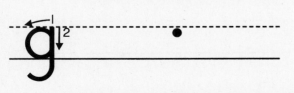

© Pearson Education, Inc.

Guess What I Am

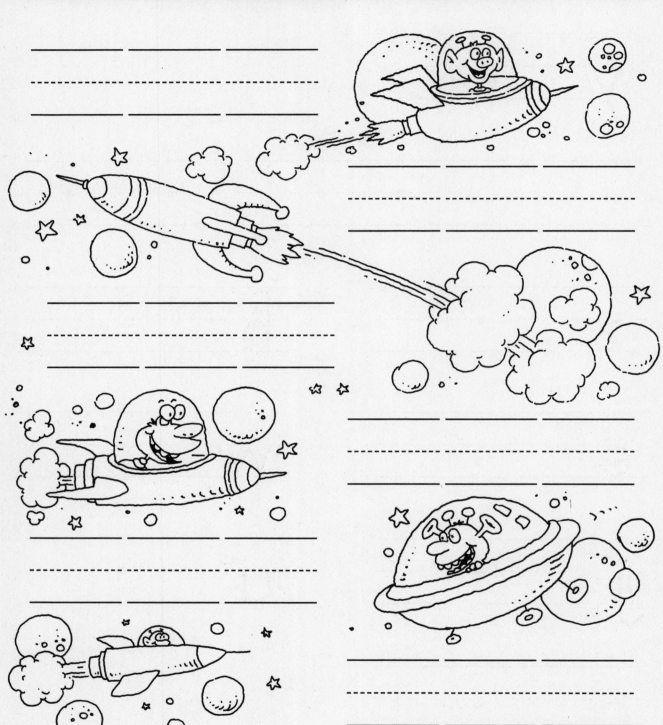

_____

- - - - - - - - - - - - - - - - - -

_____

_____

- - - - - - - - - - - - - - - - - -

_____

- - - - - - - - - - - - - - - - - -

_____

- - - - - - - - - - - - - - - - - -

_____

_____

- - - - - - - - - - - - - - - - - -

_____

© Pearson Education, Inc.

Writer's Warm-Up

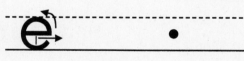

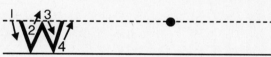

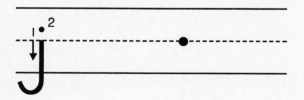

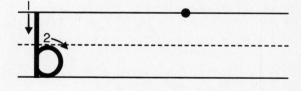

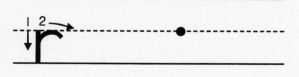

© Pearson Education, Inc.

Name _____

Word Page

____ ____ ____

---------- ---------- ----------

____ ____ ____

____ ____ ____

---------- ---------- ----------

____ ____ ____

____ ____ ____

---------- ---------- ----------

____ ____ ____

____ ____ ____

---------- ---------- ----------

____ ____ ____

____ ____ ____

---------- ---------- ----------

____ ____ ____

© Pearson Education, Inc.

Writer's Warm-Up

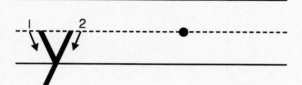

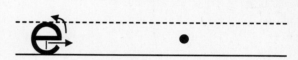

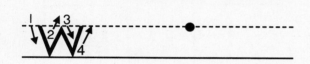

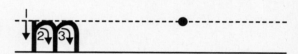

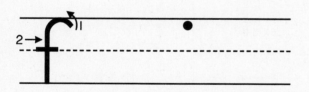

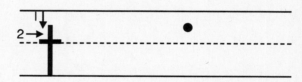

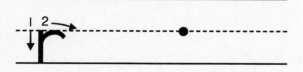

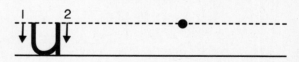

© Pearson Education, Inc.

Missing Letters

m   g

o   g

y   u

g   l

f   u

o   g

g   m

© Pearson Education, Inc.

Activity 7

Name _____

Treasure Hunt

Lesson
95

© Pearson Education, Inc.

Activity 5

Writer's Warm-Up

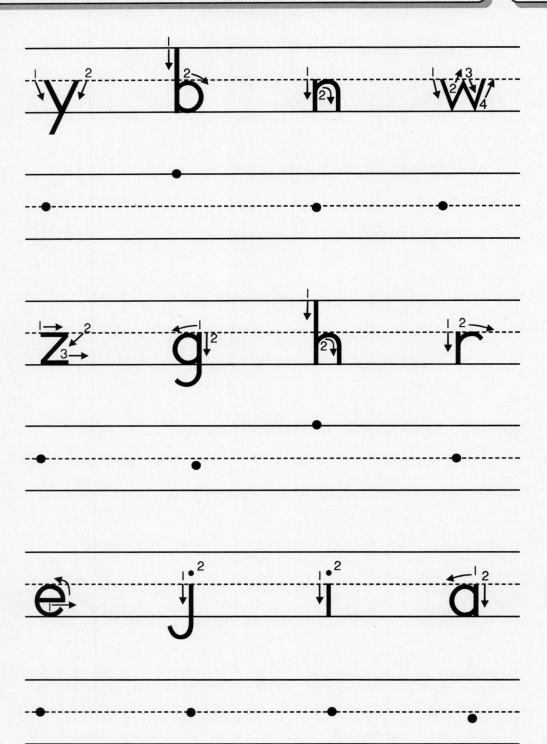

Activity 5

© Pearson Education, Inc.